DON'T DIE ON THIRD

ADVICE FOR DAILY LIVING

COMPILED BY

DAN R. CRAWFORD

Worldwide Publishing Group
7710-T Cherry Park Dr, Ste 224
Houston, Texas 77095
www.WorldwidePublishingGroup.com

ISBN: 979-8-9995694-8-6

I dedicate this book to those who have advised me, and to those who have honored me by at least listening to my advice.

Contents

INTRODUCTION

Whoever coined the phrase "Advice is cheap" was exactly right. Everywhere I've been—whatever my job, whoever my associates— I've always had people willing, even eager, to give me advice. I never had to ask for it or pay for it. It was free and quickly offered.

One day, I started thinking about all the advice I'd been given and began making a list. I thought I might collect it into a book and share my own advice with the world. Unfortunately, my memory was shorter than my list. So I sent out a note on social media asking folks to share their favorite advice from over the years. I was amazed by the response. I gathered those contributions and arranged them one per day. For the next six months, you won't have to go a single day without a helpful word. You might even pass a few choice lines along to a friend. So take my advice—enjoy the read.

What do you name a book of daily advice? My high school baseball coach, LeRoy Ashmore—until recently the winningest high school baseball coach in Texas—kept telling us, "Don't die on third!" His words were about baseball, but I heard a life lesson: finish what you start. The apostle Paul said it this way: "I have fought the good fight, I have finished the race, I have kept the faith" (2 Timothy 4:7).

When we sustained an injury, large or small, Coach would say, "Rub a little dirt on it. It'll be all right." He was talking baseball, but the line works for life, too. I've rubbed on a little "dirt" over the years, and the reason I haven't needed more is the wise counsel others have shared.

1

The contributions in this book come from family members, fellow students and former students, colleagues, church members from places where I've served as interim pastor, missionaries, pastors, church workers, and even a few folks I barely remember—but they sent in their best advice.

Read one page a day for the next six months. If you still want a daily nudge after that, start over and read it again. You may find something you missed the first time, or you can check how well you applied each day's counsel.

Hopefully, somewhere along the way, you'll say—as David said to Abigail—"Blessed is your advice" (1 Samuel 25:33).

JANUARY AND JULY

1. During the reception following our wedding, my wife's grandfather came through the line, shook my hand, and advised us, "Don't ever go to bed mad at each other," and he walked on by. I learned later that what he said was also in the Bible, "do not let the sun go down on your wrath" (Ephesians 4:26).

Advice applied today:

_____

_____

_____

_____

_____

_____

_____

_____

2. In the early years of my ministry, I got crossways with my employers, and it appeared I was about to be terminated. Rudy Hernandez gave me this advice. "If you get fired, walk out like you are leading a parade." Good advice for today or any day.

Advice applied today:

_____

_____

_____

_____

_____

_____

_____

_____

3. Sometimes I say things when I'm leading a class, and someone will say, "Wow, that's good." I don't think of it as being good advice until someone else hears it. The advice I shared was, "God does not need to be filled up by our presence, but He wants us near so we can be filled with His presence." Carolyn Ramsey was involved in the Baptist Student Ministry at East Texas State University (now East Texas A&M) when I was the Director. She was also on the search committee that called me as interim pastor at First Baptist Church, Denison, Texas.

Advice applied today:

_____

_____

_____

_____

_____

_____

_____

_____

_____

_____

4. One of my college roommates passed on the advice that life was too short not to have fun, and if friends didn't want to have fun, one should get new friends. He and I believed the same things, just with different definitions of fun.

Advice applied today:

_____

_____

_____

_____

_____

_____

_____

_____

5. I don't remember which dean said it, since I served under a lot of deans at several institutions, but someone advised the faculty, "We have excelled to a new level of incompetence." Good advice if you need it.

Advice applied today:

_____

_____

_____

_____

_____

_____

_____

_____

6. The best advice given to me in my lifetime was to be a prayer warrior. My dad was always praying for someone and reading his Bible. He taught me how I needed to intercede for others. When I pray for the needs of others, I am reminded that there are so many who have bigger needs than I do. Through the early years of marriage, motherhood, the shooting at our church, my husband's career as a police officer, issues with children and grandchildren, my two strokes, and surgeries - through it all - I have been a prayer warrior. Debbie Gillette is the Pastor's Ministry Administrative Assistant at Wedgwood Baptist Church, Fort Worth, Texas, where she has served for thirty-eight years and where I am a member.

Advice applied today:

_____

_____

_____

_____

_____

_____

_____

_____

_____

_____

7. Seven from Heaven (advice from the Old Testament): "Love the Lord your God with all your heart and with all your soul and with all your strength" (Deuteronomy 6:5).

Advice applied today:

_____

_____

_____

_____

_____

_____

_____

_____

8. As I have gotten to the age of retirement, I often think about how many times I could have just said, "Could you teach me how to do that?" or "How does that work?" and the person likely would have taken a moment to teach me or explain something. I wish I had learned how to make my grandmother's apple pie that had no

recipe. Good advice. Donna J. Wright, retired education minister, West Mobile Baptist Church, Mobile, Alabama. I worked in a nearby office when we were both employed at Southwestern Baptist Seminary.

Advice applied today:

_____

_____

_____

_____

_____

_____

_____

_____

_____

9. Advice shared with my seminary students: I will never ask you to do something I haven't either already done or am willing to do alongside you.

Advice applied today:

_____

_____

_____

_____

_____

_____

_____

_____

_____

_____

10. Advice shared with my seminary students: There are two ways to
    look good at a task: pay the price to excel or cut down everyone
    else involved.

Advice applied today:

_____

_____

_____

_____

_____

_____

_____

_____

_____

11. Eleven from Heaven (New Testament advice): "Love one another
    with brotherly affection. Outdo one another in showing honor"
    (Romans 12:10).

Advice applied today:

_____

_____

_____

_____
_____
_____
_____
_____
_____
_____

12. If you keep walking straight, eventually people can see who's walking crooked. We gave this advice to our children. Ed Markham was a preacher's kid, as was I. We met as fellow students at Howard Payne College (now University). We both married classmates - girls from the same Sunday School class at Trinity Baptist Church in San Antonio.

Advice applied today:

_____
_____
_____
_____
_____
_____
_____
_____
_____

13. The first athletic director/head football coach I worked for advised me, "Don't ever let your boss catch you at work with your hands

in your pockets." A trivial matter, to be sure, but in my thirty years of supervising coaches, teachers, and now a county road crew, I have caught myself thinking about that in evaluating personnel and giving that same advice. David Brewer is Precinct 4 Commissioner of Navarro County, Texas, and was actively involved in the Baptist Student Ministry at the University of Texas when I was the Director.

Advice applied today:

_____

_____

_____

_____

_____

_____

_____

_____

14. Never hold a grudge. Let it go and let God deal with it. Be more concerned with pressing on toward your higher calling. Chris Byrum is a teacher, a former student of mine at Southwestern Baptist Seminary, and a former church member at Rosen Heights Baptist Church, Fort Worth, when I was interim pastor.

Advice applied today:

_____

_____

_____

_____

_____

_____

_____

_____

_____

_____

15. My paternal grandfather was a career truck driver. He once gave me some advice for how to select a restaurant while traveling on the road. "To be considered for classification as a great restaurant," he said, "an eating establishment must have at least three things: (1) servings that are large; (2) tea that is sweet; and (3) a waitress that calls you, 'Honey.'"

Advice applied today:

_____

_____

_____

_____

_____

_____

_____

_____

_____

16. I have no idea where the phrase originated. Possibly it was a merger of a couple of other phrases. Sometimes you might say to someone who is struggling, "Hang in there." Other times, you might say to someone, "Be tough" or "Be strong." Somehow, I began to hear and repeat the phrase, "Hang tough!" Good advice for today.

Advice applied today:

_____

_____

_____

_____

_____

_____

_____

_____

_____

17. The emptiness and wickedness of busyness is the art of doing too much. Dr. Sharon L. Gresham, founder and director of Ashes to Crowns Ministries and member of the Board of Directors of Disciple All Nations, Inc. We first met at an area missions meeting in South Korea.

Advice applied today:

_____

_____

_____

_____

_____

_____

_____

_____

_____

18. Garbage in, garbage out. J'Nevelyn Jackson Fleming is a retired children's minister now living in Granbury, Texas. She was an active participant in the Baptist Student Ministry of East Texas State University (now East Texas A&M) when I was the Director.

Advice applied today:

_____

_____

_____

_____

_____

_____

_____

_____

19. Advice from a former teacher of mine: Why compare yourself with others? No one in the entire world can do a better job of being you than you.

Advice applied today:

_____

_____

_____

_____

_____

_____

_____

_____

_____

20. My daughter, Tabitha, and I sat together in her bedroom one evening when she was seven or eight. For some reason, the two of us came up with a saying that has stayed with us all these years: "Follow God, lead others." Good advice for anyone. Ferrell Foster is president of Kortabocker LLC and was actively involved in the Baptist Student Ministry at East Texas State University (now East Texas A&M) when I was the Director.

Advice applied today:

_____

_____

_____

_____

_____

_____

_____

_____

_____

_____

21. Advice shared with my seminary students— The most popular person in the church where you will serve is a former minister. You must live and serve in their shadow.

Advice applied today:

_____

_____

_____

_____

_____

_____

_____

_____

22. Advice shared with my seminary students: I believe in text-driven preaching, but I believe more in prayer-driven preaching. If you are not prayed up, it won't make much difference which text you use.

Advice applied today:

_____

_____

_____

_____
_____
_____
_____
_____
_____
_____

23. When I was young, I took trombone lessons (but not for long). My teacher gave good advice that went beyond music: "Don't just practice until you get it right; practice until you can't get it wrong."

Advice applied today:

_____
_____
_____
_____
_____
_____
_____
_____

24. If you are ambidextrous, be careful when hammering joists on your deck. You may end up with two blue thumbs. Donna Benner was actively involved in the Baptist Student Ministry of the University of Texas when I was Director.

Advice applied today:

_____

_____

_____

_____

_____

_____

_____

_____

25. A 1970s quote from Ralph Winter has been great advice for me over the years. He said, "What motivates me is not the possibility of successful accomplishment, but the value of the goal." Dennis Fuqua is the executive director of International Renewal Ministries and a colleague of mine on America's National Prayer Committee.

Advice applied today:

_____

_____

_____

_____

_____

_____

_____

_____

26. Sometimes the most spiritual thing you can do is take a nap—from Larry Golden, who claims it was my advice to him. Larry Golden, graduate of East Texas State University (now East Texas A&M), where I was the Baptist Student Director, was also a fellow collegiate minister. He is retired from Lifeway Christian Resources.

Advice applied today:

_____

_____

_____

_____

_____

_____

_____

_____

_____

27. Another piece of advice from my old baseball coach: "Ducks are on the pond," which in baseball meant there were runners on base and the person who was up to bat was supposed to knock them in to score. In life, the advice means everything is set up for you to succeed; all you must do is perform correctly.

Advice applied today:

_____

_____

_____

_____

_____

_____

_____

_____

_____

_____

28. In leadership it is better to spend more time with fewer people than with more people. Josh Arrington, lead pastor, Church on the Rock Global Ministries, Pitt Meadows, British Columbia, Canada. His wife, Lisa, was a former student of mine at Southwestern Baptist Seminary.

Advice applied today:

_____

_____

_____

_____

_____

_____

_____

_____

29. Remember, if they talk to you about them, they will talk to them about you. Mike Davenport, member of First Baptist Church,

Denison, Texas where I was interim pastor; former member of the Board of Directors, Disciple All Nations, Inc.

Advice applied today:

_____

_____

_____

_____

_____

_____

_____

_____

30. After a two-and-a-half-year battle with cancer, my mother lay peacefully in bed. She looked at me with calm assurance and advised me by saying, "Everything is going to be fine." In that moment—despite the deep pain and looming grief of impending loss—I was fully convinced that she genuinely believed what she said. Her quiet confidence bore witness to her unwavering trust that, in the end, Jesus always brings about what is good, even through suffering. Vidal Muñiz, specialist in Texas Baptists en Español and my co-host on "Discipleship Directives" podcasts.

Advice applied today:

_____

_____

_____

_____

_____

_____

_____

_____

_____

_____

31. Always have a best friend at every age level. Dr. Al Fasol, Distinguished Professor of Preaching (retired), Southwestern Baptist Seminary, and a former faculty colleague of mine.

Advice applied today:

_____

_____

_____

_____

_____

_____

_____

_____

FEBRUARY AND AUGUST

1. When my parents took me off to college and unloaded most of my worldly possessions into my dorm room, my Dad had one last word of advice: "Just remember who you are." While those were years of discovery as to my identity, I never forgot that who I was becoming was a result of who I was.

Advice applied today:

_____

_____

_____

_____

_____

_____

_____

_____

2. "If someone makes you an offer that requires money and brains, they will run out of brains about the time you run out of money." Advice from my grandfather.

Advice applied today:

_____

_____

_____

_____

_____

_____

_____

_____

3. Integrity is not always easy or popular, but it is always right. Challenges will come from many directions. We must face each one with determination to do the right thing for the right reasons, always based on His truth. Dr. Joyce Ashcraft was actively involved in the Baptist Student Ministry at East Texas State University (now East Texas A&M) when I was the Director. She was also a colleague, co-worker, and member of the Board of Directors, Disciple All Nations, Inc.

Advice applied today:

_____

_____

_____

_____

_____

_____

_____

_____

_____

_____

4. If an opportunity comes along, consider it fully, and if it is a good opportunity, accept it. Bernard Whitney is an attorney in Fort Worth and a member of Rosen Heights Baptist Church, where I was interim pastor. He is also on the Board of Directors of Disciple All Nations, Inc.

Advice applied today:

_____

_____

_____

_____

_____

_____

_____

_____

_____

5. Don't do too good on a really bad job, or you'll never get to do anything else. Dr. Bob McEachern, International Mission Board personnel and friend from volunteer mission trips.

Advice applied today:

_____

_____

_____

_____

_____

_____

_____

_____

6. Years ago, when I was leading music for a number of evangelists in revivals around the country, a pastor shared with me some advice by Mark Antony in his funeral oration for Julius Caesar: "The evil that men do lives after them; the good is oft interred with their bones." I typed this into a small sign that I have kept on my various desks throughout the years. Denton McDugle, long-time business owner and politician, my high school friend and first college roommate.

Advice applied today:

_____

_____

_____

_____

_____

_____

_____

_____

_____

_____

7. Seven from Heaven (advice from the Old Testament). "Choose a good reputation over great riches; being held in high esteem is better than silver or gold" (Proverbs 22:1–2).

Advice applied today:

_____

_____

_____

_____

_____

_____

_____

_____

8. I now appreciate the people who taught without me asking (because I wouldn't have asked). The lawyer in my first job taught me about land plats, deeds, liens, wills, and titles—even though he knew I would only work there for one year. I have used that information my entire life. Donna J. Wright, retired education minister, West Mobile Baptist Church, Mobile, Alabama. I worked in a nearby office when we were both employed at Southwestern Baptist Seminary.

Advice applied today:

_____

_____

_____

_____

_____

_____

_____

_____

9. Advice shared with my seminary students—So live that when the negative rumors swirl around you, no one will believe them.

Advice applied today:

_____

_____

_____

_____

_____

_____

_____

_____

10. Advice shared with my seminary students—When uninformed on a subject, it is best to remain silent during a discussion and let others think you know nothing than to open your mouth and prove it.

Advice applied today:

_____

_____

_____

_____

_____

_____

_____

_____

11. Eleven from Heaven (New Testament advice). "Whatever you do, work heartily" (Colossians 3:23).

Advice applied today:

_____

_____

_____

_____

_____

_____

_____

_____

_____

_____

12. The best way to listen to the Lord is to go to the site of the prayer concern, or to the person for whom you are praying. This gives God opportunity to respond directly to our focus. Lewis Turner followed a career in the U.S. Army with teaching and writing involvement through Wheatland Ministries.

Advice applied today:

_____

_____

_____

_____

_____

_____

_____

_____

_____

13. I was preaching at a small church in Austin while a student at U.T. and was advised to give only one great thing to think about in my sermon. I retorted, "I will come up with many great ideas in every sermon. Why limit myself to one great idea per sermon?" I was reminded of the KISS acronym: "Keep It Simple, Stupid." One great idea per sermon is an admirable goal. It shaped the way I preach. This advice applies to all of life: Keep It Simple, Stupid.

Eddie Hogan is pastor of the First Methodist Church of Ore City, Texas, and was actively involved in the Baptist Student Ministry at the University of Texas when I was the Director.

Advice applied today:

_____

_____

_____

_____

_____

_____

_____

_____

_____

14. After I had miscarried our first baby, we were dumbfounded and grieving the loss. About a week later a letter came to us from a pastor friend. Very simple letter with his prayer and advice to us: "I pray that this will not make you bitter but make you better." Brenda (Colvin) Marsh. Actively involved in the Baptist Student Ministry of the University of Texas when I was Director.

Advice applied today:

_____

_____

_____

_____

_____

_____

_____

_____

_____

_____

15. Dr. Jimmie Nelson was the acting dean of the doctoral programs at Southwestern Baptist Seminary when I applied to be admitted to the doctoral program. I knew going in it was a big risk, since my undergraduate and graduate grades were not very good. He spent a long time looking over my transcripts before he spoke. Then he said, "You know, Crawford, all I can say is that you have a lot of guts, applying for a doctoral program." I made him a promise that if I made a B in any seminar, I would drop out automatically. He agreed, and thanks in part to his advice, today they call me Dr. Crawford.

Advice applied today:

_____

_____

_____

_____

_____

_____

_____

_____

16. Steve Longcrier is a huge fan of General Thomas "Stonewall" Jackson, so his bit of advice comes from the general: "Always look people in the face when addressing them and generally when they address you." Steve is the founder and executive director of Civil War Heritage Trails and was actively involved in the Baptist Student Ministry at the University of Texas when I was the Director.

Advice applied today:

_____

_____

_____

_____

_____

_____

_____

_____

17. Years ago, Daddy and our neighbor Mr. Jordan were hanging over the back fence chatting. I walked out to let Daddy know dinner was ready. He wrapped up his conversation with Mr. Jordan, and we walked to the house. He told me, "Sister, that was a sad tale. He's been working an assembly line his whole life and hated every minute of it. Promise me that you won't let that happen." Good advice. Linda McMillan is the database manager at Texas Wesleyan University and a friend from the Fort Worth Cats minor league baseball days.

Advice applied today:

_____

_____

_____

_____

_____

_____

_____

_____

18. Look for the good to focus on (because God is good). J'Nevelyn Jackson Fleming is a retired children's minister, now living in Granbury, Texas. She was an active participant in the Baptist Student Ministry of East Texas State University (now East Texas A&M) when I was the Director.

Advice applied today:

_____

_____

_____

_____

_____

_____

_____

_____

19. Decide ahead of time that you will forgive anyone who may hurt or wrong you in any way. Experiencing hurt from others is unavoidable. By consciously choosing to forgive, you conserve energy, avoid unnecessary grief and sleepless nights, and invite more joy and peace into your life. This approach exemplifies the way of Jesus and carries its own unique blessings. Hamish and Cindy Buntain, Salt Spring Island, British Columbia, Canada. Recently retired regional ministry leader for British Columbia. During a six-month sabbatical leave spent teaching at the Canadian Southern Baptist Seminary in Alberta, Canada, he was my pastor.

Advice applied today:

_____

_____

_____

_____

_____

_____

_____

_____

_____

20. Teaching my kids how to drive, I found myself saying, without previous thought to do so, "Don't let the person behind you drive your car." Good advice for drivers and others. Ferrell Foster is president of Kortabocker LLC and was actively involved in the Baptist Student Ministry at East Texas State University (now East Texas A&M) when I was the Director.

Advice applied today:

_____

_____

_____

_____

_____

_____

_____

_____

21. Advice shared with my seminary students—Always dress just a little bit above the level of your church members, but not too much. They might cut your salary.

Advice applied today:

_____

_____

_____

_____

_____

_____

_____

_____

22. Advice shared with my seminary students—I believe in exegeting the Scripture in order to preach or teach, but you also better exegete your audience; otherwise, you'll be saying all the right things to the wrong group.

Advice applied today:

_____

_____

_____

_____

_____

_____

_____

_____

_____

23. Advice from a coach I once had—Stop keeping score once the game is over.

Advice applied today:

_____

_____

_____

_____

_____

_____

_____

_____

_____

_____

24. A piece of advice came from my mother. Whenever I was working on a project or task and became frustrated, she said to just walk away for a little while. Then come back, and you can look at it with a fresh attitude, and you will be calmer, which helps your thinking. Donna Benner was actively involved in the Baptist Student Ministry of the University of Texas when I was Director.

Advice applied today:

_____

_____

_____

_____

_____

_____

_____

_____

25. If you are a stranger to prayer, you are a stranger to the greatest source of power known to human beings. Deborah (DeeJay) Van is a twenty-five-year Texas law enforcement officer, and a member of The Bridge FBC Rio Hondo, Texas, and a Valley Baptist Missions Education Center student of mine.

Advice applied today:

_____

_____

_____

_____

_____

_____

_____

_____

26. When I said, "I can't be a summer missionary. I've hardly been out of Texas," the advice I was given was, "Why don't you let God decide?" Dr. Hal F. Cunnyngham, emeritus missionary, International Mission Board, SBC; forty years; served as Journeyman and career missionary in Taiwan and East Asia and staff member in the home office. Former student, involved in the Baptist Student Ministry at East Texas State University (now East Texas A&M), when I was the Director.

Advice applied today:

_____

_____

_____

_____

_____

_____

ADVICE FOR DAILY LIVING

---

27. "Life is too short to fish with a dead minnow" is fishing advice given by a father to a son when the son continued to fish with a dead minnow on his hook in order to save money by buying expensive live minnows. The fishing advice became life advice for the son—redeem the time God has given us on earth and let Him make it productive for His glory. Mickey Porter, the son, is from Pampa, Texas, but traveled the world before settling in Layton, Utah.

Advice applied today:

---

28. "Seize the day" has been our family saying, started by my husband, Oscar Turner. Claire Turner Lawrence is one of my longest-

standing friends, since we met at age nine in the children's ministry of the same church.

Advice applied today:

_____

_____

_____

_____

_____

_____

_____

_____

29. (August and February during leap year.) Never date someone you would not marry. You never know when you might fall in love. Sylvia Stephens Watkins, college classmate of mine at Howard Payne University.

Advice applied today:

_____

_____

_____

_____

_____

_____

_____

_____

_____

_____

30. (August) If you can do anything besides ministry and be happy, do it. Allen Bramlett, pastor, Trinity Hills Baptist Church, Benbrook, TX. I preceded him as interim pastor.

Advice applied today:

_____

_____

_____

_____

_____

_____

_____

_____

31. (August) My daddy told me from the time I was a little girl that your word is your bond. If you said you were going to do something, it was as good as done! Sandra McCurdy, librarian and prayer partner.

Advice applied today:

_____

_____

_____

_____

_____

_____

_____

_____

_____

_____

_____

MARCH AND SEPTEMBER

1. My aunt taught seventh-grade Texas history all her career. In my early teenage years, I would visit her and sit in on her classes. She told me once, "Always be proud that you are a Texan. Not everyone is so fortunate." Having been in all fifty states and lived outside of Texas, I realize that every place has its own pride, and without being obnoxious to others, my pride was in Texas, and I tried to keep the advice of my aunt.

Advice applied today:

_____

_____

_____

_____

_____

_____

_____

_____

_____

2. "Watch the pennies, and the dollars will take care of themselves." Being raised by parents who survived the Depression, I was

brought up to be thrifty, but this expression has often reminded me not to be wasteful. Jeff Sadler is owner of Sadler Properties in Lawton, Oklahoma, and a member of First Baptist Church, Lawton, where I was interim pastor on two occasions.

Advice applied today:

_____

_____

_____

_____

_____

_____

_____

_____

3. Life is usually a matter of perspective. No matter what you see when you look at a situation, there is another perspective. Our response must be to let God shape our perspective and use that to accomplish His purpose and plan. Dr. Joyce Ashcraft was actively involved in the Baptist Student Ministry at East Texas State University (now East Texas A&M) when I was the Director. She went on to serve in the collegiate ministry area of the Baptist General Convention of Texas. She also serves on the Board of Directors, Disciple All Nations, Inc.

Advice applied today:

_____

_____

_____

_____

_____

_____

_____

_____

4. You never stand taller than when you kneel in prayer. Glenn Sheppard, President/CEO at International Prayer Ministries, served on the staff of the North American Mission Board at the same time I was on the staff.

Advice applied today:

_____

_____

_____

_____

_____

_____

_____

_____

5. It will be better tomorrow. From my mother, a registered nurse. Her advice was almost always correct.

Advice applied today:

_____

_____

_____

_____

_____

_____

_____

_____

_____

6. Go out of your way to help others. Suzanne Perry, minister to international students, University of British Columbia, Vancouver, British Columbia, Canada, and my former graduate assistant during her student days at Southwestern Baptist Seminary.

Advice applied today:

_____

_____

_____

_____

_____

_____

_____

_____
_____
_____

7. Seven from Heaven (advice from the Old Testament). "Delight yourself also in the Lord, and He shall give you the desires of your heart" (Psalm 37:4).

Advice applied today:

_____
_____
_____
_____
_____
_____
_____
_____
_____

8. "People who love Jesus do what He says. People who do what He says have read in His book what to do." Dr. Bob McEachern, International Mission Board personnel and friend from volunteer mission trips together.

Advice applied today:

_____
_____
_____

_____

_____

_____

_____

_____

_____

_____

9. Plan for the day you might have to retire earlier than planned—physically, spiritually, and emotionally. Some things have a much greater impact on changes in our lives than financial loss. Think about how you will purposely adjust to sudden new directions. Contributor was an active participant in the East Texas State University (now East Texas A&M) Baptist Student Ministry when I was Director. They describe themselves as an "Anonymous longtime educator by God's design!"

Advice applied today:

_____

_____

_____

_____

_____

_____

_____

_____

10. Advice shared with my seminary students (those whom I was sending to preach spring revival meetings)—The degree to which the congregation accepts you will be largely dependent on the introduction of you that the pastor shares, so dress up and be nice to him when he picks you up at the airport.

Advice applied today:

_____

_____

_____

_____

_____

_____

_____

_____

11. Eleven from Heaven (New Testament advice). "Let every man be swift to hear, slow to speak, slow to wrath" (James 1:19).

Advice applied today:

_____

_____

_____

_____

_____

_____

_____

_____

_____

_____

12. You can't minister to people unless you know the people. Like coaching, you can't coach someone unless you know how or what they need to be coached. R.D. (Ricky) Fowler, a long-time friend from Southwestern Baptist Seminary where Bill King passed on this advice to him. He has been pastor of Bethel Baptist Church in Lincoln, Nebraska, for thirty-four years.

Advice applied today:

_____

_____

_____

_____

_____

_____

_____

_____

_____

13. Advice shared with my seminary students—It's better to be rejected for who you are than be accepted for who you are not.

Advice applied today:

_____

_____

_____

_____

_____

_____

_____

_____

14. When possible, do not handle receiving any cash in any transaction in business or ministry where there is no paper trail. Not only will it be a temptation to pocket it, but this action is just poor practice. Keep in mind that even if you do not mishandle funds, just the speculation or rumors of mishandling is damaging. Dr. Joe Hernandez, retired missionary/missions administrator/seminary and college professor; actively involved in Baptist Student Ministry at Pan American University (now University of Texas Rio Grande Valley) when I was Director.

Advice applied today:

_____

_____

_____

_____

_____

_____

_____

_____

_____

_____

15. Act like you've been there. (Advice offered in response to undignified behavior by athletes when they start winning.) William Woo, teacher at Calvary Baptist School, La Verne, CA, and a former student of mine at Southwestern Baptist Seminary.

Advice applied today:

_____

_____

_____

_____

_____

_____

_____

_____

16. One of my favorite seminary professors was Dr. Cal Guy. He opened every missions class by reading a letter from a missionary. After one letter, in which the missionary explained that a particular program had been tried without success several times, but every time they voted to discontinue it, the women missionaries would block-vote and keep it in use, Dr. Guy folded the letter and put it

back in his notebook, then said, "You know, if killing cats were up to women, the world would be three feet deep in cats." The guys in the class had a great laugh. The girls, not so much. Still, it was not bad advice.

Advice applied today:

_____

_____

_____

_____

_____

_____

_____

_____

17. Choose your battles wisely and always ask yourself, "Is this a hill worth dying on?" Vicki J. Lee, a member of the First Baptist Church in Graham, Texas, where I supplied the pulpit on a number of occasions, during a difficult time in the life of their church.

Advice applied today:

_____

_____

_____

_____

_____

_____

_____

_____

_____

_____

18. The ones who don't do their homework are the ones who need to do their homework the most. From my tenth-grade Latin teacher. Toby Shockley, Crossroads Christian Fellowship and Mountain Time Ministries, and former student of mine at Southwestern Baptist Seminary.

Advice applied today:

_____

_____

_____

_____

_____

_____

_____

_____

_____

19. Advice from a preacher I heard once—Never be afraid to try; remember… amateurs built the ark; professionals built the Titanic.

Advice applied today:

_____

_____

_____

_____

_____

_____

_____

_____

20. Remember who and Whose you are. J'Nevelyn Jackson Fleming is a retired children's minister, now living in Granbury, Texas. She was an active participant in the Baptist Student Ministry of East Texas State University (now East Texas A&M) when I was the Director.

Advice applied today:

_____

_____

_____

_____

_____

_____

_____

_____

21. When you go to vote, you're never voting for Jesus. In other words, no political candidate is perfect, and you will not agree with anyone completely. Now, that said, some candidates are downright evil and in it only for themselves. Beware of such people. They may smile pretty and say some things you like, but they're dangerous. "Wolves in sheep's clothing" comes to mind. In fact, policies are not the most important thing about a candidate to me; the most important thing is his or her character. Ferrell Foster is president of Kortabocker LLC and was actively involved in the Baptist Student Ministry at East Texas State University (now East Texas A&M) when I was the Director.

Advice applied today: Advice applied today:

_____

_____

_____

_____

_____

_____

_____

_____

_____

22. Advice shared with my seminary students—When your church has a covered-dish dinner, you'd better eat a little bit of everything. There is a little old lady watching you.

Advice applied today:

_____

_____

_____

_____

_____

_____

_____

_____

23. My high school basketball coach once yelled his advice to us during a practice session: "Shoot the d##### ball; you can't make a basket dribbling the ball." Good life advice.

Advice applied today:

_____

_____

_____

_____

_____

_____

_____

_____

24. Advice shared with my seminary students—God's call to ministry remains even if you disobey. Close by every rejection of God's call is a large fish, waiting to be God's protection until you respond correctly.

Advice applied today:

_____

_____

_____

_____

_____

_____

_____

_____

25. The advice "You're only as old as you feel" may have been derived from a 1927 sermon from Rev. Clarence H. Wilson of the Flatbush Congregational Church in New York as he encouraged his audience to adopt a youthful perspective. "How old would you be if you didn't know how old you were?" he asked. That question was later made popular by Major League Baseball player Satchel Paige.

Advice applied today:

_____

_____

_____

_____
_____
_____
_____
_____
_____
_____

26. Sometimes a project doesn't turn out the way you planned. Don't call it a problem; view it as an opportunity. Donna Benner, actively involved in the Baptist Student Ministry of the University of Texas when I was Director.

Advice applied today:

_____
_____
_____
_____
_____
_____
_____
_____

27. "Do more for others than they can do for you!" Harry Chavanne was a friend of my Dad's and the father of my long-time friend, Claire Chavanne Lawrence.

Advice applied today:

_____

_____

_____

_____

_____

_____

_____

_____

28. Blessed are the flexible, for they shall not be bent out of shape. Doug Loafman's advice from his mother, Luci Loafman. I knew both of them when I served twice as interim pastor of Central Baptist Church in Livingston, Texas. Doug went on to become pastor of Union Baptist Church in El Dorado, Arkansas.

Advice applied today:

_____

_____

_____

_____

_____

_____

_____

_____

29. Never give up. (Taken from a young boy with cancer, and made it her own motto.) Betty Nance, fellow church member at Wedgwood Baptist Church, Fort Worth, TX.

Advice applied today:

_____

_____

_____

_____

_____

_____

_____

_____

30. You can never finish unless you start. Steve Williams, pastor, chaplain, former student at Southwestern Baptist Seminary, Fort Worth, TX.

Advice applied today:

_____

_____

_____

_____

_____

_____

_____

_____

_____

_____

31. (March) When you introduce yourself to someone, pay attention. Don't be mentally preparing your next comment, or you won't remember their name two minutes later. Bob Sheffield, pastor and denominational worker, father of Lynn Sheffield Barker, who was actively involved in the Baptist Student Ministry at the University of Texas when I was Director.

Advice applied today:

_____

_____

_____

_____

_____

_____

_____

_____

APRIL AND OCTOBER

1. My favorite college professor said one day in a class of wannabe ministers, "Boys, if you resign and leave your church position to get away from a problem, you will run into two problems in your next church position." He was a wise man with wise advice.

Advice applied today:

_____

_____

_____

_____

_____

_____

_____

_____

_____

2. My pastor-father warned me not to be like some preachers who were like cross-eyed javelin throwers—they didn't get much distance, but they did keep people alert. Advice worth hearing and applying.

Advice applied today:

_____

_____

_____

_____

_____

_____

_____

_____

3. Years ago, when we were raising our girls, my husband, Gil, would tell them when using a knife, "Always cut toward yourself." His advice was dead wrong, but it made it memorable, and they always remembered not to do that. Sally Lemon Machost and husband Gil were members of Central Baptist Church, Livingston, Texas, where I served twice as interim pastor.

Advice applied today:

_____

_____

_____

_____

_____

_____

_____

_____

_____

_____

4. My Momma always said, "If you want to be a sweet little old lady, you'd better start now!" Melinda Massey, retired elementary school teacher. She was a member of First Baptist Church, Lawton, Oklahoma, where her husband, Ralph, was on the ministerial staff and I was interim pastor on two occasions.

Advice applied today:

_____

_____

_____

_____

_____

_____

_____

_____

5. Always be sure the brake on your brain is engaged before putting your mouth in motion! Patti Irby, fellow church member at Wedgwood Baptist Church, Fort Worth.

Advice applied today:

_____

_____

_____

_____

_____

_____

_____

_____

_____

_____

6. Start with your best and stay with it. University of Texas legendary football coach Darrell Royal said it this way—"We've got to dance with who brung us." Of course, he was talking about football, but the advice applies.

Advice applied today:

_____

_____

_____

_____

_____

_____

_____

_____

7. Seven from Heaven (advice from the Old Testament). "They who wait for the Lord shall renew their strength; they shall mount up with wings like eagles; they shall run and not be weary; they shall walk and not faint" (Isaiah 40:31).

DON'T DIE ON THIRD

Advice applied today:

_____

_____

_____

_____

_____

_____

_____

_____

8. Always be at the right place at the right time with the right equipment. Mark Dawson (advice from my band director), fine arts accompanist at Ector County Independent School District (Texas), was actively involved in the Baptist Student Ministry at the University of Texas when I was the Director.

Advice applied today:

_____

_____

_____

_____

_____

_____

_____

_____

69

9. Advice shared with my seminary students (those whom I was sending to preach spring revival meetings)—Satan has a great track record in three areas: sex, power, and money. You will arrive at your destination with a target on your back.

Advice applied today:

_____

_____

_____

_____

_____

_____

_____

_____

10. Advice shared with my seminary students—Don't ever talk to people about God until you've talked to God about the people.

Advice applied today:

_____

_____

_____

_____

_____

_____

_____

_____

_____

11. Eleven from Heaven (New Testament advice). "Let your conduct be without covetousness" (Hebrews 13:5).

Advice applied today:

_____

_____

_____

_____

_____

_____

_____

_____

_____

12. Our coaches always told us, "Early is on time, on time is late, and late is unacceptable." Good advice. Rashel Stevens is administrative assistant at Oak Grove Baptist Church in Burleson, Texas, where I served as interim pastor.

Advice applied today:

_____

_____

_____

_____

71

_____

_____

_____

_____

_____

_____

13. Keep your mouth closed when painting the ceiling. Donna Benner, actively involved in the Baptist Student Ministry of the University of Texas when I was Director.

Advice applied today:

_____

_____

_____

_____

_____

_____

_____

_____

14. I once heard a teacher give this advice: If serving is beneath you, then leadership is beyond you.

Advice applied today:

_____

_____

_____

_____

_____

_____

_____

_____

_____

_____

15. My maternal grandfather owned a grocery store, a gas station, and a real estate office, and was the first postmaster for Bellmead, Texas, a suburb of Waco. From the age of two to five, I lived with him and my grandmother (Father in Germany for WWII; Mother in a sanitarium with tuberculosis). He was a steward in the Christian Church on Sunday mornings and a frequent attender of the Baptist church on Sunday evenings. He said he attended the Christian church because he "liked the preaching, but disliked the 'German' music," and he attended the Baptist church because "he liked the music, but disliked the preaching." When I became a pastor of a small church, he called me every Sunday night at 10 p.m. to get a report on my day. Best accountability partner I ever had, and his advice was always spot-on.

Advice applied today:

_____

_____

_____

_____

_____
_____
_____
_____
_____
_____

16. When I told my parents that I was going to ask my girlfriend to marry me, my father said to consider that you are not just marrying the girl but her whole family also. Her family made great in-laws. Dr. Gary W. Loudermilk, retired pastor and director of missions and classmate of mine in doctoral seminars.

Advice applied today:

_____
_____
_____
_____
_____
_____
_____
_____

17. Buy low and sell high. Rocky Feemster is a partner with Touchstone Bernays Law Firm in Dallas. He was actively involved in the University of Texas Baptist Student Ministries while I was the Director.

Advice applied today:

_____

_____

_____

_____

_____

_____

_____

_____

18. My high school basketball coach, Steven Smith, taught his players about life as much as he taught them about the game of basketball. He said, "This game comes with rules; if you wanna play the game, you're gonna play by the rules." Buck Pate is technical manager for Holt Cat and is an active member of Trinity Hills Baptist Church in Benbrook, TX, where I was interim pastor. He is also on the Board of Directors for Disciple All Nations, Inc.

Advice applied today:

_____

_____

_____

_____

_____

_____

_____

_____

_____

_____

19. My dad used to say to us regularly on his way out the door, "Hold the fort," meaning take care of things until I return. Good advice. Dr. Craig O'Brien is pastor of Origin Church, on the campus of the University of British Columbia, Vancouver, BC, Canada. He is also a former student of mine at Southwestern Baptist Seminary.

Advice applied today:

_____

_____

_____

_____

_____

_____

_____

_____

_____

20. What immediately comes to mind for me is some advice from my mechanical engineering professor, circa 1973, that has served me well throughout my career. He said, "If it looks wrong, it ain't right." Stan Kelly is a stress analyst engineer at BWX Technologies, Inc. (Virginia/Florida), and was actively involved in the Baptist Student Ministries at the University of Texas when I was the Director.

Advice applied today:

_____

_____

_____

_____

_____

_____

_____

_____

21. Advice shared with my seminary students—If someone hands you an announcement on your way into the auditorium on Sunday morning, be very, very careful. It could be a half-truth, and you may get the incorrect half.

Advice applied today:

_____

_____

_____

_____

_____

_____

_____

_____

22. Advice shared with my seminary students—God's call on your life must be settled at the start; otherwise there will be mornings that you can't get up and go to work.

Advice applied today:

_____

_____

_____

_____

_____

_____

_____

_____

23. It's not what you know; it's who you know that really makes a difference. I must have at least a hundred examples of this.

Advice applied today:

_____

_____

_____

_____

_____

_____

_____

_____

_____

24. Remember, marriage is based on your commitment and not your feelings. Feelings come and go, up and down. Commitment is steadfast and there no matter what. Brenda (Colvin) Marsh. Was actively involved in the Baptist Student Ministry of the University of Texas when I was Director.

Advice applied today:

_____

_____

_____

_____

_____

_____

_____

_____

_____

25. Measure twice, cut once. Working in the remodel field, you had to check your work before you reached the point of no return because once a mistake was made you couldn't just make it disappear. Billy Manning was a member of the staff at the University of Texas Baptist Student Ministry with me and a member of Oak Grove Baptist Church, Burleson, Texas, when I was interim pastor. He is also on the Board of Directors for Disciple All Nations, Inc.

Advice applied today:

_____

_____

_____

_____

_____

_____

_____

_____

26. A friend from another culture once told me, "Everyone smiles in the same language." Good advice to smile at someone today.

Advice applied today:

_____

_____

_____

_____

_____

_____

_____

_____

27. After I finished teaching a Bible study on wisdom, the oldest member of our church came up to me and said she had a piece of advice to share. She said, "Don't think just because you bring your children to church, they will follow the Lord." Debbie Boucher is the retired minister of missions and ministry at Valley Grove Baptist Church in Stephenville, Texas, where I served as interim pastor.

Advice applied today:

_____

_____

_____

_____

_____

_____

_____

_____

28. Third base can be a scary place. Let God be your third-base coach. He will get you home. Joel Salazar is associate pastor of music/worship at First Baptist Church, Grand Prairie, Texas. Prior to that he was minister of music/worship at Central Baptist Church in Livingston, Texas, where I was interim pastor two times.

Advice applied today:

_____

_____

_____

_____

_____

_____

_____

_____

_____

29. Don't let your passport expire. (This is really an application of the Boy Scout motto I learned as a young man: "Be prepared.") Dr. Tom Hearon, missionary. He was under my supervision during doctoral study at Southwestern Baptist Seminary.

Advice applied today:

_____

_____

_____

_____

_____

_____

_____

_____

30. If you are the smartest person in the room, find a new room. Kirby Basham is superintendent of schools, Grandview, Texas, and a

member of First Baptist Church, Grandview, when I was interim pastor.

Advice applied today:

_____

_____

_____

_____

_____

_____

_____

_____

_____

31. (October) Never steal someone's joy. Accept gifts, compliments, and a drink with a smile and a Southern, "You're so sweet. Thank you." Melissa Stearman is a member of Trinity Hills Baptist Church, Benbrook, TX, where I was interim pastor.

Advice applied today:

_____

_____

_____

_____

_____

_____

_____

_____

_____

_____

_____

MAY AND NOVEMBER

1. My sixth-grade teacher, Mrs. Merle Acton, used to say in class, "There is greatness in this class." Every time she said that, I remember looking around at my classmates and thinking she might be talking about me. I've long since lost contact with everyone in that class, so I have no idea if anyone achieved "greatness," but I do know that her advice motivated me for many years after sixth grade.

Advice applied today:

_____

_____

_____

_____

_____

_____

_____

_____

2. During my teenage years, while still living at home, I would frequently hear the following advice from my mother as I left the house at night: "Nothing much good happens after midnight."

Advice applied today:

_____

_____

_____

_____

_____

_____

_____

_____

_____

3. Never trust a spiritual leader that doesn't limp. (Based on the story of Jacob walking away with a limp after wrestling with God.) Toby Shockley, Crossroads Christian Fellowship and Mountain Time Ministries, and former student of mine at Southwestern Baptist Seminary.

Advice applied today:

_____

_____

_____

_____

_____

_____

_____

_____

_____

_____

4. "There is always just the right word to express the exact thought you wish to convey. But you must be intentional to find it!" This is the advice of an older friend, the historian in our church, shared with his grandsons—my best friends during preteen and early teenage years.

Advice applied today:

_____

_____

_____

_____

_____

_____

_____

_____

_____

5. Don't fall back down and away from an inside fastball, because it will strike you behind the ear and knock you out. Personal experience of Dr. Bob McEachern, International Mission Board personnel and friend of mine from volunteer trips.

Advice applied today:

_____

_____

_____

_____

_____

_____

_____

_____

6. Just be yourself, but be a team player. Advice from Fred Lawrence, long-time friend, whom I first met when we were nine years old. Retired, living in Cypress, Texas.

Advice applied today:

_____

_____

_____

_____

_____

_____

_____

_____

7. Seven from Heaven (advice from the Old Testament). "Honor your father and your mother, that your days may be long in the land" (Exodus 20:12).

Advice applied today:

_____

_____

_____

_____

_____

_____

_____

_____

_____

8. Save it for the things that matter. Debbie Butler Gilbert (advice given to her about marriage), high-school teacher, counselor, and principal, Mesquite Independent School District. She was actively involved in the Baptist Student Ministry at East Texas State University (now East Texas A&M) when I was the Director.

Advice applied today:

_____

_____

_____

_____

_____

_____

_____

_____

_____

_____

9. Advice shared with my seminary students (those whom I was sending to preach spring revival meetings)—A fifty-minute sermon will not prove how intelligent you are, but a twenty-five-minute sermon will win you a lot of new friends.

Advice applied today:

_____

_____

_____

_____

_____

_____

_____

_____

10. Advice shared with my seminary students—If you hear that I have a need, don't you dare send your prayers to me. Wrong direction. I can't do anything with those prayers except appreciate your concern. Send your prayer about me to God.

Advice applied today:

_____

_____

_____

_____

_____

_____

_____

_____

11. Eleven from Heaven (New Testament advice). "Do nothing from selfish ambition or conceit, but in humility count others more significant than yourselves" (Philippians 2:3).

Advice applied today:

_____

_____

_____

_____

_____

_____

_____

_____

12. I once heard a counselor offer this advice to a small group: As the rest of the world is walking out the door, your best friends are the ones walking in.

Advice applied today:

_____

_____

_____

_____

_____

_____

_____

_____

13. Never make fun of your spouse's choices, because you were one of them. Steve Bravo was actively involved in the Baptist Student Ministry at the University of Texas when I was the Director.

Advice applied today:

_____

_____

_____

_____

_____

_____

_____

_____

_____

_____

14. "Remember who you are" was advice passed on to Larry Golden by his pastor-father. Interestingly enough, that was the same advice passed on to me by my pastor-father. Larry Golden, graduate of East Texas State University (now East Texas A&M), where I was the Baptist Student Director, was also a fellow collegiate minister. He is retired from Lifeway Christian Resources.

Advice applied today:

_____

_____

_____

_____

_____

_____

_____

_____

15. Every morning from kindergarten through high school, my mother walked me out of the front door of our house with this advice: "Do the best you can, with what you have, for Jesus' sake today." I googled to see where that quote came from and found several

opinions. As far as I was concerned, it came from my mother. When I went away to college, I missed it greatly.

Advice applied today:

_____

_____

_____

_____

_____

_____

_____

_____

16. Dr. Jesse Northcutt was one of my preaching professors at Southwestern Baptist Seminary, and one day in class he reminded all of us that when pastoring a church, we would always encounter disagreements or arguments. He went on to advise us that most are usually meaningless, so choose carefully about our involvement. Dr. Gary W. Loudermilk, retired pastor and director of missions and classmate of mine in doctoral seminars.

Advice applied today:

_____

_____

_____

_____

_____

_____

_____

_____

_____

_____

17. Don't cross against the light. Rocky Feemster is a partner with Touchstone Bernays Law Firm in Dallas. He was actively involved in the University of Texas Baptist Student Ministries while I was the Director.

Advice applied today:

_____

_____

_____

_____

_____

_____

_____

_____

_____

18. My high school basketball coach, Steven Smith, taught his players about life as much as he taught them about the game of basketball. He said, "Your teammates rely on you to carry your part. You can't do it without them, and they can't do it without you. Love it when both of you fulfill your responsibilities." Buck Pate is technical

manager for Holt Cat and is an active member of Trinity Hills Baptist Church in Benbrook, TX, where I was interim pastor. He is also on the Board of Directors of Disciple All Nations, Inc.

Advice applied today:

_____

_____

_____

_____

_____

_____

_____

_____

19. You can't go wrong doing right. I gave that line to classmate Ray Hilderbrand, and he wrote a good song and recorded it. Ed Markham was a senior yell leader at Howard Payne College (now University) responsible for freshman initiation. I was a freshman at the same school. Amazingly, we are still friends.

Advice applied today:

_____

_____

_____

_____

_____

_____

_____

_____

_____

_____

20. If you fail, never give up, because F.A.I.L. means "First Attempt In Learning." End is not the end; in fact, E.N.D. means "Effort Never Dies." If you get "no" as an answer, remember N.O. means "Next Opportunity." Jerry Kline is the pianist at New Hope Baptist Church in Mansfield, Texas, where I was interim pastor.

Advice applied today:

_____

_____

_____

_____

_____

_____

_____

_____

_____

21. Advice shared with my seminary students—If your town has a Fourth of July parade, you would do well to ride on the fire truck.

Advice applied today:

_____

_____

_____

_____

_____

_____

_____

_____

22. Advice shared with my seminary students—You can dress up or dress down when you preach or teach; just remember that the message is more important than the messenger.

Advice applied today:

_____

_____

_____

_____

_____

_____

_____

_____

23. I was having lunch one day with a fellow minister when he passed on the following advice: You will only change people by your lifestyle, never by your opinion.

Advice applied today:

_____

_____

_____

_____

_____

_____

_____

_____

_____

24. The Baptist student minister at Bee County College advised me to "Go to seminary." I didn't know what that was, and my family was opposed to it, but I went. It was like being advised to take the next step, even when parts of it are unknown. It was good advice. Rose Zamora, retired teacher; former employee with Mission Arlington, Southern Baptist WMU, and Texas Baptist WMU. We served together on the Alumni Board of Directors at Howard Payne University.

Advice applied today:

_____

_____

_____

_____

_____

_____

_____

_____

_____

_____

25. "Don't count your chickens before they hatch." Advice my father gave me when I was a boy. We raised chickens, and he was incubating a batch of eggs. I counted them up and proudly announced, "We're going to have [my count] new chickens!" The well-used saying stayed with me throughout my life. It taught me to be cautiously optimistic—to stay hopeful, but always mindful of potential downsides. John Chaloupka is a CPA in Bedford, Texas, and a member of Shady Oaks Baptist Church, Hurst, Texas, when I was interim pastor. He is also on the Board of Directors of Disciple All Nations, Inc.

Advice applied today:

_____

_____

_____

_____

_____

_____

_____

DON'T DIE ON THIRD

26. The relationship between you and God is just that, and nobody else gets a say in it. Elaine Woodward Rocholl was actively involved in the Baptist Student Ministries at Pan American University (now University of Texas Rio Grande Valley) when I was the Director.

Advice applied today:

_____
_____
_____
_____
_____
_____
_____
_____
_____

27. My dad, a coach, advised me, "Don't let anyone outwork you." Sharon Rush Graves was former secondary ELA curriculum coordinator in Crowley, Texas, and instructional coach at Houghton Mifflin Harcourt. She obviously took her father's advice and played basketball at Baylor University. She was a member of Oak Grove Baptist Church in Burleson, Texas, where I was interim pastor.

Advice applied today:

_____

_____

_____

_____

_____

_____

_____

_____

28. My dad advised me, "When you go to a barbershop, pick the barber with the worst haircut, because one of the other barbers did that." Clark Dunlap is the former pastor at First Baptist Church Smithfield, North Richland Hills, Texas, and currently discipleship pastor at Calvary Baptist Church, Rosenberg, Texas. He is a former student of mine at Southwestern Baptist Seminary.

Advice applied today:

_____

_____

_____

_____

_____

_____

_____

_____

_____

29. Advice from a school superintendent—"Never be the first to try something new, but never be last either." David Brewer is Precinct 4 Commissioner at Navarro County, Texas, and was actively involved in the Baptist Student Ministry at the University of Texas when I was the Director. He is also a member of the Board of Directors of Disciple All Nations, Inc.

Advice applied today:

_____

_____

_____

_____

_____

_____

_____

_____

_____

30. If you always tell the truth, you never have a hard time keeping your story straight. Jay Grigg from his father, Jasper Grigg—both members of First Baptist Church, Lawton, OK, when I was interim pastor twice.

Advice applied today:

_____

_____

_____

_____

_____

_____

_____

_____

31. (May) Embrace the small moments. Our life is filled with them, but they are fleeting. Rebecca Greever Oaxaca, daughter of Jack Greever, my collegiate ministry colleague and boss.

Advice applied today:

_____

_____

_____

_____

_____

_____

_____

_____

JUNE AND DECEMBER

1. Get people praying for you. Sometimes you cannot pray for yourself. Ellen O'Brien works as a learning specialist with dyslexic students and an educator trainer with Education Mavericks, and serves the Lord with Origin Church in Vancouver, British Columbia, where her husband, Craig, is the pastor. She was also a student of mine at Southwestern Baptist Seminary.

Advice applied today:

_____

_____

_____

_____

_____

_____

_____

_____

_____

2. I spent a couple of summers as a camper at Ozark Boys Camp and Baseball School in Mt. Ida, Arkansas (now a coed summer camp called Camp Ozark), and another two summers as a

counselor/coach. The co-owner of the camp was a rough, gruff-talking Arkansas hillbilly baseball player who consistently punctuated the games by yelling, "Be an Oriole!" Most of us had no clue what that meant, but we assumed it meant to work harder and do a better job at baseball. Years later I looked it up and found: "Its striking colors and melodious songs make the Oriole a symbol of joy, optimism, and positive energy." So it was good advice, after all.

Advice applied today:

_____

_____

_____

_____

_____

_____

_____

_____

_____

3. My grandmother Mary Will Rogers told me this when she was around ninety-one years old. She said that her high-school French teacher had encouraged her to drink two glasses of water first thing every morning when she got up. For as long as I can remember, my grandmother did so. She lived to be 103 and still had her memory and was in fairly good health... I guess the advice that her French teacher gave her in 1927 probably helped her live until her

103rd birthday. Merrie Lewis Smith, former student of mine at Southwestern Baptist Seminary.

Advice applied today:

_____

_____

_____

_____

_____

_____

_____

_____

4. "While steering anything, keep your head on a swivel, focus on your surroundings, and anticipate problems before they become real." Advice shared by the foreman after I got Uncle Bill's Ford tractor stuck in a steep ditch while mowing his pasture. Fred Lawrence has been my friend since we were in the Children's Ministry together at our church in Houston.

Advice applied today:

_____

_____

_____

_____

_____

_____

_____

_____

_____

_____

5. My dad always said, "Life is uncertain, eat your dessert first, and don't buy any green bananas." J'Nevelyn Jackson Fleming is a retired children's minister now living in Granbury, Texas. She was an active participant in the Baptist Student Ministry of East Texas State University (now East Texas A&M) when I was the Director.

Advice applied today:

_____

_____

_____

_____

_____

_____

_____

_____

6. "That's no hill for a high stepper." As a child growing up, this is something my mom would say to encourage us children when faced with a challenge. Sue Wallace is retired but works at Blessing Funeral Home in Mansfield, Texas. She is also a member

of New Hope Baptist Church in Mansfield, Texas, where I was interim pastor.

Advice applied today:

_____

_____

_____

_____

_____

_____

_____

_____

7. Seven from Heaven (advice from the Old Testament). "Iron sharpens iron, and one man sharpens another" (Proverbs 27:17).

Advice applied today:

_____

_____

_____

_____

_____

_____

_____

_____

8. I've told young people who came to work with me at various Christian nonprofits: "Don't sell your soul to this organization; sell your soul to Jesus. As long as this organization helps you serve God, then you're in a good place. If it stops being so, well, you know what to do." Ferrell Foster is president of Kortabocker LLC and was actively involved in the Baptist Student Ministry at East Texas State University (now East Texas A&M) when I was the Director.

Advice applied today:

_____

_____

_____

_____

_____

_____

_____

_____

9. Advice shared with my seminary students—As a minister, you will be one of the most popular people in town, and when you leave your popularity will increase considerably.

Advice applied today:

_____

_____

_____

_____

_____

_____

_____

_____

_____

_____

10. Advice shared with my seminary students—The worst word in private prayer is "Amen," because it means you are finished. God may not be finished yet.

Advice applied today:

_____

_____

_____

_____

_____

_____

_____

_____

11. Eleven from Heaven (New Testament advice). "Do not grow weary of doing good, for in due season we will reap, if we do not give up" (Galatians 6:9).

Advice applied today:

_____

_____

_____

_____

_____

_____

_____

_____

12. Help children discover who God uniquely made them rather than pushing your will on their life. Gayla Brown Greeson lives in Richmond, Texas, and works for Community Bible Study. She was actively involved in the Baptist Student Ministry at the University of Texas when I was the Director.

Advice applied today:

_____

_____

_____

_____

_____

_____

_____

_____

13. It is best never to be alone with a person of the opposite sex in a car, in a building, or anywhere you are not in the company of others. Place windows in your office so that people inside the building can see you and anyone in the office with you. Once again, even if nothing inappropriate might have happened, just the speculation or rumors—or a person in your setting who may misrepresent what might have or have not occurred—is damaging. Dr. Joe Hernandez, retired missionary/missions administrator/seminary and college professor; actively involved in Baptist Student Ministry at Pan American University (now University of Texas Rio Grande Valley) when I was Director.

Advice applied today:

_____

_____

_____

_____

_____

_____

_____

_____

_____

_____

14. My driver's-education instructor told us not to be intimidated by other drivers or allow them to make us speed, especially if they honk or tailgate. He said we should focus on driving correctly and following the rules of the road because the driver is responsible for everyone in the car. I have always kept this in mind and believe it

applies to the Christian life as well as driving. We must keep our focus on the rules God set out for us and not be swayed or intimidated by what the world says. Donna Benner was actively involved in the Baptist Student Ministry of the University of Texas when I was Director.

Advice applied today:

_____

_____

_____

_____

_____

_____

_____

_____

15. Another of my favorite seminary professors was Dr. Roy Fish, who a few years later became a faculty colleague and a friend. When I joined the faculty, he gave me this advice concerning serving as an interim pastor: "Get your interims as far away as possible. You will work less and they will pay you more." Among thirty interims, I have served as far away as 260 miles and as close as eight miles. He was right.

Advice applied today:

_____

_____

DON'T DIE ON THIRD

_____

_____

_____

_____

_____

_____

_____

_____

16. At the age of five I had been invited to a birthday party. My mom and I shopped for a gift and finally settled on a book. When the day came for the party I told my mom I wanted to keep the book. She knew this was one of those teachable moments. She didn't scold me, but explained that the Bible says "it is more blessed to give than to receive." We went to the party, and that was the first time I understood that concept. I have never forgotten her advice to me. Rhonda Childs Woods—was actively involved in the Baptist Student Ministry at East Texas State University (now East Texas A&M) when I was the Director.

Advice applied today:

_____

_____

_____

_____

_____

_____

_____

_____

_____

_____

17. "Hit 'em where they ain't." Linda McMillan remembered this advice from the character Annie Savoy in the movie *Bull Durham*. Actually this was a quote from William "Wee Willie" Keeler, who was a right fielder in Major League Baseball from 1892 to 1910. Applied to real life, it is good advice. Linda is a friend from season-ticket days with the Fort Worth Cats minor-league baseball team.

Advice applied today:

_____

_____

_____

_____

_____

_____

_____

_____

18. My high school basketball coach, Steven Smith, taught his players about life as much as he taught them about the game of basketball. He said, "ALWAYS do your best to position yourself so you can clearly see the goal." Buck Pate is technical manager for Holt Cat and is an active member of Trinity Hills Baptist Church in

Benbrook, TX, where I was interim pastor. He is also on the Board of Directors of Disciple All Nations, Inc.

Advice applied today:

_____

_____

_____

_____

_____

_____

_____

_____

_____

19. My grandmother, in her Texas accent, advised me, "Do what you can, and can what you can't." In other words, move on from those things over which you have no control. JD Templeton was former pastor at Cotton Center First Baptist Church in Cotton Center, Texas, and is currently minister of adult discipleship at Trinity Baptist Church, Kerrville, Texas. He is a former student of mine at Southwestern Baptist Seminary.

Advice applied today:

_____

_____

_____

_____

_____

_____

_____

_____

_____

_____

20. Things might be hard now, but keep climbing that mountain and learning. Then someday that mountain will be far away, and you can be proud you didn't give up. Jerry Kline is the pianist at New Hope Baptist Church in Mansfield, Texas, where I was interim pastor.

Advice applied today:

_____

_____

_____

_____

_____

_____

_____

_____

21. Advice shared with my seminary students—If you forget to make a crucial announcement during the worship service, it is OK to include it in the closing prayer.

Advice applied today:

_____

_____

_____

_____

_____

_____

_____

_____

_____

22. I have received and shared the following advice of Charles Spurgeon: "Brother, if any man thinks ill of you, do not be angry with him. For you are worse than he thinks you to be." Paul Gustafson is a registered kinesiotherapist and was actively involved in the Baptist Student Ministry at the University of Texas when I was the Director.

Advice applied today:

_____

_____

_____

_____

_____

_____

_____

_____

_____

_____

23. My truck-driver grandfather once passed on this advice—If you can't dazzle them with your brilliance, baffle them with your bull. (Only he used another word at the end of his advice.)

Advice applied today:

_____

_____

_____

_____

_____

_____

_____

_____

24. My mother advised me, "Don't you break that boy's heart." Cynthia Dement Cunnyngham. Married to Dr. Hal F. Cunnyngham for almost fifty years; emeritus missionary—International Mission Board, SBC. Forty years of missionary service. Served as Journeyman to Brazil, career missionary in Taiwan and East Asia, and staff member in the home office. Former student, involved in the Baptist Student Ministry at East Texas State University (now East Texas A&M) when I was the Director.

Advice applied today:

_____
_____
_____
_____
_____
_____
_____
_____

25. "Play it where it lies" is the golf equivalent of what Paul wrote in Philippians 4:11: "Whatever state I am, [I have learned] to be content." We cannot always change our circumstances, but we can adjust to them. I've hit many a golf shot that I would like to pick up and improve my "lie," but that is not allowed. Neither can I change my life circumstances. So, I play it where it lies, and advise others to do the same.

Advice applied today:

_____
_____
_____
_____
_____
_____

_____

_____

_____

26. Don't ever turn down a chance to serve due to not being ready, even if the service interrupts previous plans. Advice shared with me by Dr. John R. Campbell, retired director of missions, Nacogdoches, Texas.

Advice applied today:

_____

_____

_____

_____

_____

_____

_____

_____

27. My advice is that sometimes people don't need any advice. As I lead in GriefShare, I learned that the lion's share of my time should be spent listening. Grieving people often have lots of people telling them what they ought to do—what they need more is a caring and compassionate listener who will give them time to process their grief. Donna J. Wright, retired education minister, West Mobile Baptist Church, Mobile, Alabama. I worked in a nearby office when we were both employed at Southwestern Baptist Seminary.

Advice applied today:

_____

_____

_____

_____

_____

_____

_____

_____

28. Advice from my wise father-in-law—"I never learned very much with my mouth open." Dr. Gerry Lewis is the retired executive director/lead strategist for Harvest Baptist Association in Texas and currently the church engagement officer for Texans on Mission. He is a former student of mine at Southwestern Baptist Seminary.

Advice applied today:

_____

_____

_____

_____

_____

_____

_____

_____

_____

29. Don't burn any bridges. (Advice from her father.) Rosie Horvath, career piano teacher and fellow member of Wedgwood Baptist Church, Fort Worth, Texas.

Advice applied today:

_____

_____

_____

_____

_____

_____

_____

_____

30. A person can only do so much in a day. Kelsey Granberry, owner, Granberry Title, LLC, and active member of the Baptist Student Ministry at the University of Texas when I was Director there.

Advice applied today:

_____

_____

_____

_____

_____

DON'T DIE ON THIRD

_____

_____

_____

_____

_____

31. (December) If you can't get it all done in a 24-hour day, work
    nights. Jeff Sadler is owner of Sadler Properties in Lawton,
    Oklahoma, and a member of First Baptist Church, Lawton, where
    I was interim pastor on two occasions.

Advice applied today:

_____

_____

_____

_____

_____

_____

_____

_____

BITS OF ANONYMOUS
LEFT-OVER ADVICE

- Many people have gone farther than they thought they could because someone else thought they could.

- If it sounds too good to be true, it probably isn't true.

- Somewhere, someone is sitting in the shade today because someone planted a seed long ago.

- A bend in the road is not the end of the road unless you fail to make the turn.

- You can't live a positive life with a negative attitude.

- You can't pour from an empty cup.

- If you want the rainbow, you've got to put up with the rain.

- It is better to take many small steps in the right direction than to make a great leap forward only to stumble backward.

- When you feel like quitting, think about why you started.

- You can never cross the ocean unless you have the courage to lose sight of the shore.

- There is no "I" in team.

- If you get up one more time than you fall, you'll make it through.

- ✓ Never tell me the sky is the limit when there are footprints on the moon.

- ✓ Don't miss all the beautiful colors of the rainbow while looking for the pot of gold.

- ✓ If you can't run with the big dogs, stay on the porch.

- ✓ Every great achievement was once impossible.

- ✓ An obstacle may be either a stepping stone or a stumbling block.

- ✓ He who wants milk should not sit himself in a pasture and wait for a cow to back up to him.

- ✓ Do what you need to do now. Sometimes "later" becomes "never."

- ✓ The early bird may get the worm, but that doesn't speak well for the early worm.